THINK SMALL

HouseBeautiful

THINK SMALL

MAKE THE MOST OF EVERY SQUARE FOOT

HEARST BOOKS

New York

Dressed up in a collage of hand-painted 18th-century Chinese wallpaper, an 8-by-8-foot bedroom sleeps three: designer David Kaihoi, his wife, and their young daughter. "The trundle bed only comes out at night, and gets pushed back under the bed first thing in the morning, so for all practical purposes we never really see it," he explains.

THE
LUXURY
OF
LESS

"The way to stay happy when
you're living on top of one
another is by ruthlessly editing—
one thing in, one thing out.
A place for everything,
and everything in its place."
—DAVID KAIHOI

One of the most impactful strategies for making small quarters live—and look—larger is to edit your surroundings. The following spaces exemplify a streamlined approach to décor and possessions, from pared-back palettes to minimalist accessorizing. If you think "less" means "sacrifice," think again. "A smart thing to do in small spaces is limit your number of gestures," says Susan Ferrier. "That is to say, you must have huge gestures, but just a few of them, repeated throughout; it's the repetition of similar imagery that calms a space."

Doing away with extraneous furnishings boosts functionality and navigability. It also reduces visual clutter and injects white space, a favorite designer trick. Can one piece—a storage ottoman, a daybed—perform the role of two? Could your desk double as a dining table? Sometimes just deaccessioning an underutilized accent chair renders cramped quarters more expansive. "You've got to leave some breathing room," explains Maxwell Gillingham-Ryan. "Emptiness allows the eye to travel someplace and rest. Every space will feel bigger if you leave some things out." That dictum also applies to decorative accents. Consider storing some and rotating your displays. Not only will you gain usable surface area, you'll see your collections with fresh eyes when it's their turn in the spotlight.

An edited approach to hues and materials can go a long way, too. Just a few coordinating tones, versus a riot of colors and patterns, create calm and cohesiveness in petite confines. But you needn't eschew fun prints. "Do the whole room—walls, curtains, upholstery, even the lampshades and picture frames—in the same fabric, whether leopard or toile," says Amanda Nisbet. "One wild print all over the place enlarges a small space, makes it feel cohesive, and adds a big wow factor." There's a certain joy and freedom in limiting yourself: "You don't have to do 50 things to make a house beautiful," says Robert Stilin. "You make choices and edit."

MAKE A ROOM SERVE MANY PURPOSES

In the entry of his West Hollywood house, Mark Egerstrom built a Douglas fir gallery shelf that cantilevers off the staircase to double as extra seating for the glass-topped table: "It functions as an entry center table, a serving table, a breakfast table, and, with a linen cloth, a formal dining table."

PARED-BACK PALETTES

Soothe the eye and create a calming ambience. A tightly edited selection of color, materials, and even architectural details also imparts continuity, making cramped conditions feel more expansive.

> "A tightly edited palette is important to make all the patterns work together."
>
> —KRISTA EWART

WHITEWASH EVERYTHING (right)
In the dining area of a California beach cottage, Krista Ewart doused a set of 1960s chairs in the same milky hue as the surrounding architecture. "White makes them disappear into the walls—it's less busy and helps open the space—but still lets you see the super cool design."

USE WOOD FINISHES TO CALM (opposite)
David Netto used a complement of wood tones in the dining area of a Swedish-inspired Long Island cottage. His choice of Charlotte Perriand rush chairs and a rough-hewn table that match the exposed woodwork—in white-washed pine—ensures that the space reads cozy rather than claustrophobic.

MATCH FURNITURE TO THE WALLS (*above*)
Though a banquette extends the length of this dining room, it doesn't overwhelm because the faux suede is the same tone as the wall paint. "I like the biggest pieces of furniture in a room to disappear or blend into the wall," says designer Benjamin Dhong. A glass-topped dining table likewise keeps the room from feeling jumbled.

SIMPLIFY ARCHITECTURAL DETAILS (*right*)
Lindsey Bond Meadows streamlined every aspect of her modestly sized 1950s cottage—including trim and woodwork. "I removed the mantel to keep things crisp and fresh. Unless they're fabulous, mantels and moldings are just clutter," she says. "To me, a running horizontal line of shelves looks like the horizon—so peaceful. Floating shelves are a great way to make spaces airy without a bunch of furniture."

"Pristine white, clean lines, symmetry, neatness: That's what I call serenity."
—LINDSEY BOND MEADOWS

THE BIGGER THE BETTER

Conventional wisdom suggests using dainty furnishings in snug quarters, but designers often recommend the opposite strategy: Use bigger pieces—an optical illusion that makes the room read larger. But avoid the urge to overfurnish, and use just a few larger-scale items.

GO FOR MAJOR DRAMA (above)
An enormous Baroque pine cartouche from Austria is repurposed as a headboard for the tiny bedroom of a Salt Lake City guesthouse. "You don't have to have a lot of pieces in a room if the pieces have a lot of character," explain designers Marshall Watson and Jeffrey Kilmer.

MIX BIG AND SMALL (opposite)
Nick Olsen took an iconoclastic route in kitting out a 295-square-foot Brooklyn studio with a mix of large and more modestly proportioned pieces, including a love seat and Louis XV–style chair. "You've got to bring in a few overscale elements because these are the bold moves that make a room," he says. "Forget the rules: People think that every piece of furniture has to be pint-size."

DO MORE WITH LESS

Why use two furnishings when one will perform double-duty? These must-have multitaskers combine many functions—so the room can, too.

RELAX—OR REST— ON DAYBEDS *(top)*
When the bedrooms of her Marin County, California, cottage are filled up, Kim Dempster's living room sleeps one more—courtesy of a super-deep Victorian settee that is a favorite spot for afternoon naps, too.

ÉTAGÈRES OFFER COPIOUS STORAGE *(bottom)*
Mediating between the adjacent living room and kitchen, Melanie Pounds's Birmingham, Alabama, dining room gets copious use—as does her étagère, a workhorse that stores dishes, displays heirlooms, holds mail, and transforms into a buffet during parties.

1. STOOLS WORK AS SIDE TABLES, TOO These use-'em-anywhere wonders work as supplementary perches or an extra surface to stash books or drinks. Krista Ewart designed this polka-dotted pair to service a window seat in her sister's beach house. "I have the same ones in my own home. They're great for extra seating and take up so little space. I tuck mine under a side table next to my sofa and just pull them out when I need to." **2. CARD TABLES AREN'T JUST FOR CARDS** A 1970 Karl Springer table in one corner of a parlor by Kevin Isbell invites bouts of backgammon and cards, or can be used as an intimate dining vignette. **3. SECRETARIES COMBINE STORAGE AND WORK SURFACE IN ONE** Libby Cameron used a flip-down desk to hide a home office in a client's master bedroom. **4. OVERTAKING A SLIVER OF SPACE** in David Kaihoi's 390-square-foot one-bedroom, an antique gentleman's chest has multiple personalities: desk, bar, child's bureau, and—when the child was in diapers—changing table.

A TREASURE OF POSSESSIONS

Downsizing doesn't have to mean sacrificing style—or deaccessioning all your favorite possessions. Although most people use relocation as an excuse to pare down to the essentials, an intrepid few embrace an aesthetic of abundance to squeeze more into less space.

> "We British turn everything into something else—curtains become upholstery, upholstery becomes pillows. Here, I had the pictures reframed and sofas reshaped and sized."
>
> —ALEXANDER DOHERTY

GIVE OLD PIECES NEW LIFE

A linen-strewn daybed is equally suited to sleeping or lounging in a petite guest room. "This apartment is almost 1,000 square feet smaller than where my clients had been living. And that place was jammed to the gills with Chinese export ceramics, midcentury modern furniture, American abstract paintings," says Alexander Doherty. "My role was to edit, to make a boatload of stuff cohesive and pleasing to the eye."

DON'T GIVE UP Relocating from a ten-room Dallas house to a four-room apartment, Craig Schumacher was loath to part with his many collections. "I didn't want to give up anything, so my look just became layered and more layered," he says. To wit: his tiny study, installed cheek-to-jowl with prized antiques. "I really don't have a decorating philosophy except to make everything I love fit wherever I am."

GET CREATIVE

Downsizing to a smaller house, Kevin Isbell's client didn't want to part with her beloved 12-foot-long sofa. To accommodate it in the new living room, Isbell had to put it against a wall with a doorway; hanging a 19th-century sorcerer's mirror above distracts from the unusual placement.

DOWNSIZING? *Some words from the wise.*

"Minimalism is very difficult to do well in a small space. You have to maintain things more rigorously."

—BILL BROCKSCHMIDT

"In a small space the visual message has to be simple and straight forward, or it becomes chaotic. You need a simple overarching design narrative; we try to tell one story."

—ANDREW HALLIDAY & DAVID GREER

"Edit down to the things you totally love. I told myself, 'you get to hang one big piece of art in the living room.'"

—KELLY GIESEN

"I'm single and my kids are grown, so a smaller house makes sense. And you actually use every room. I wanted a dining room, a library, a den, and an office, but I didn't have that kind of space. I had to make it all work in one room."

—CHRIS BARRETT

"We have these great examples of living stylishly in small spaces: Stanley Barrows, Van Day Truex, Billy Baldwin—they made it an art form. They had these jewel boxes that they redecorated every three or four years, and the space became a laboratory for their ideas."

—MAUREEN FOOTER

"[A salon-style installation] makes a hallway feel like a place and not just a thoroughfare."

—ELLEN O'NEILL

"Choose one set of dishes for all occasions, one sauté pan, and one set of glasses— those stemless wine glasses work for juice, cocktails, wine, milk. Live only with what you love and use daily. Think of it as a different kind of abundance."

—CLARE DONOHUE

"I know so many people who have three dens. When I ask them how they want to use their rooms, they have no idea. Each space has to have a purpose to come alive."

—MELANIE POUNDS

Mary Douglas Drysdale was so charmed by her client's hand-painted childhood furniture that she copied its floral motif on the walls of the 8-by-9-foot bedroom that houses it. "We duplicated the flower design on an inexpensive bed, and we created a variation to paint on the walls." The restrained hues and repetition of patterns quiet tight quarters.

CORNERS ARE OFTEN OVERLOOKED

But they are best put to work in small spaces. (Indeed, super-small rooms are practically all corners!) One designer go-to is an L-shape banquette or sectional, which provides ample seating area in a streamlined package—while taking full advantage of these underutilized nooks.

A BIG SOFA FOR A TIGHT PINCH *(left)*
For her Missouri lake house, Rhoda Burley Payne chose a chenille-covered sectional to encourage hard-core lounging. "We shoe-horned a large geranium-red sofa into this small room, for groups to relax on and watch a movie."

MAKE ROOM FOR SITTING *(opposite)*
Thom Filicia transformed his upstate New York getaway into "a cozy retreat where we can hide from the world." Board-and-batten walls confer intimacy in the den, where a corner sectional maximizes space and abets frequent entertaining.

"I go to people's houses that are twice the size of mine and there's not enough seating, there's a lot of seating here."

—THOM FILICIA

USE THIS, NOT THAT!

Good things do come in small packages. Swap space-hogging furniture and fixtures for more diminutive (or multipurpose) alternatives.

Use under-cabinet refrigerators—or refrigerator drawers—instead of a full-size model, like this airy Chicago galley by Richard Bories and James Shearon. This is an especially effective trick for kitchens that are open to adjacent living areas.

Follow Maureen Footer's lead and use a small drop-leaf in place of a large dining room table. By day, it functions as a side table; by night, with a crisp tablecloth, it's ideal for one-on-one meals.

Take a cue from Stephen Shubel's low-ceilinged living room and use a pair of stools in lieu of an oversize coffee table. Their smaller footprint makes the room more navigable, and they can be pulled a bit closer to the armchairs to better service them.

Try a tall table in place of a fixed kitchen island, as Chris Barrett did in a kitchen nook "too small for a dining table and too big for nothing." The 1860s Czech antique serves as both breakfast island and buffet for dining on the adjacent terrace.

ADAPTABLE DÉCOR

Reinvent your rooms daily—or hourly—to support different activities via transformable or mobile furnishings. Added bonus: Constant rearranging keeps your eye engaged with the space, making rooms appear larger. Even something as simple as refreshing accessories can do the trick.

WHEELED WONDERS *(right)*
In the small study of an Upper East Side townhouse by Michael Smith, a Regency-style chair near the window sits on casters for easy repositioning.

SWAP A BIG TABLE FOR A CLUSTER OF STOOLS *(opposite)*
The living room of Mark Egerstrom's 1,200-square-foot West Hollywood home commingles a tufted-leather sofa with a mélange of stools, from a stump table of his own design to Philippe Starck's vase-shape La Bohème. "Use small tables instead of big coffee tables, which eat up a room," he says. "Being able to move things around makes you feel less beholden and cramped."

LIVE AND DINE IN ONE ROOM *(right)*
To open up space in his living room, David Kaihoi built a velvet-covered corner banquette, with hidden storage beneath the seats. A nearby console—actually an Empire-style card table with its leaves folded down—converts into the dining table at night. "In such a small apartment, everything has to have more than one purpose," he explains.

SEATS OFFER MAXIMUM FLEXIBILITY *(opposite)*
"I like small chairs that feel flexible—slipper chairs in particular—otherwise a room can feel static, foreboding," says Pat Healing, who opted for lots of little seats in this airy salon. Other space-enlarging strategies inject airiness: an abundance of pale, watercolor-inspired neutrals, a Lucite coffee table, and light-reflective surfaces.

ANATOMY OF A HOME

The key to making design consultant Ellen O'Neill's New York studio apartment feel airy was to edit, edit, edit—from the color palette to possessions—and arrange furniture to create mini rooms.

"The idea of one perfectly proportioned room really appealed to me. I just wanted a modern cubicle, where I could recline on a daybed and touch everything."

—ELLEN O'NEILL

1 **HEADROOM AND VIEWS IMBUE EXPANSIVENESS** "With this 10-foot ceiling and the big, windowed doors and the terrace, it doesn't feel small at all."

2 **BE ATTENTIVE TO SCALE** The custom daybed was tailored to the exact dimensions of this tranquil studio. "I wanted it to have a certain scale and not look like a bed made into a daybed," she explains.

3 **CHOOSE PIECES THAT MULTITASK** "The efficiencies I learned when I was designing luxury hotel rooms helped when it came to furnishing. I have pieces that multitask: The daybed serves as both seating and a bed, my antique farm table serves as a desk and dining table." Even the Ingo Maurer chandelier doubles as an overhead bulletin board.

4 MULTIPLE SEATING AREAS "The various randomly placed chairs create 'lobby moment' conversation. The club chairs are very small-scale—very narrow, very 'lady.'"

5 KEEP COLORS QUIET "I knew from the start that I wanted a black-and-white palette. But just black and white can be too hard and cold, too optical. You need some creams and grays and sepias to ease you into a softer, gentler world and add a little romance."

6 HARDWORKING PIECES Located at the far end of the living area, O'Neill's farm table–desk does double duty as a dining table when she entertains. A huge mirror leaning against the wall reflects light and adds the illusion of more space.

7 PURGE POSSESSIONS (*but only to a point*) Leaving behind a six-and-a-half-room apartment for this studio, O'Neill was ruthless about streamlining her possessions: "I had a huge sale. It was a pretty healthy purge. I kept my books, my black-and-white tablecloth, and a few sentimental bits. It lasted about four days! I felt so naked, it was almost like I didn't have clothes on. I really needed my papers and things."

LAST WORDS

Play against type and use generously proportioned pieces in tight quarters.

"If you put something big in [a small room], everybody walks in and immediately says, 'Oh, wow, this space is really big.' Your eye plays tricks on you. I like big things that really make a statement—but just a few of them, otherwise it becomes overpowering."

—KERRY DELROSE

"Plus, a small room usually feels better with big furnishings."

—GARY MCBOURNIE

"Don't be afraid of major statements in a small space: a substantial sofa, large artworks, Navajo rugs, and other bold geometric patterns."

—MARK EGERSTROM

"Big furniture makes a small space seem grander."

—DAVID KAIHOI

"I like large, substantial pieces. They make a small space feel more solid and important. Overscale furniture kind of fools you into thinking the space is bigger than it is. It's a great old illusionary trick. Small furniture in small rooms only emphasizes that they're small. A large-scale piece gives the room oomph and adds dimension."

—KEN FULK

"One big accessory has more impact than a bunch of miniatures."

—KRISTA EWART

"Rotate accessories. I have many beautiful objects but I don't put them out all over the house all the time."

—MOISES ESQUENAZI

"Bigger pieces trick your eye into thinking a smaller room is actually bigger."

—AMANDA NISBET

"Don't be afraid of using big pieces in small rooms; they enhance the sense of spaciousness and scale."

—FRANCES SCHULTZ

SWITCH-HITTER A tiny space between the walk-in steam room and the garden of designer Stephen Shubel's Sausalito cottage multitasks as a lounge, study, and guest quarters, courtesy of a storage-incorporating daybed deep enough to accommodate a twin-size tufted mattress.

CHOOSE TRANSFORMABLE FURNITURE David Greer and Andrew Halliday designed tiny guest quarters for a client's 900-square-foot aerie. "It's a multi-purpose room: It also functions as a study and a den," explains Greer. "It's a very tight little space, but the floating desk is actually attached to a pier with metal clips, and when you lift it off, there's enough room to pull out the sofa bed."

FUNCTION
FIRST

"Built-in cabinets can make
even the most restricted spaces
seem expansive. In a small
space, a wall has to be put to
work." —ANDREW HALLIDAY
& DAVID GREER

unctionality is a key attribute of any room, no matter the size, but it's paramount in tight quarters. A space that works well can live and look much larger than it is, whereas one with clunky circulation, subpar storage, or an impractical furniture plan risks feeling cramped. These environments exhibit space-saving tricks and strategies that render snug quarters more navigable, comfortable, and chic to boot.

Attention to circulation is one way to make a major impact: Bodies need enough wiggle room to maneuver in. Avoid overcrowding a room with furnishings, and consider pieces with rounded or curved profiles versus sharp corners, plus seating with low (or no) arms. Pieces should also be properly scaled: small enough that they're not out of proportion to their surroundings, but large enough to comfortably accommodate users.

How furniture is arranged—and how easily it can be rearranged—affects a room's usability, too. It's often prudent to push sofas and large items against walls, but the opposite can work wonders in certain cases. Putting furniture in the center of a room frees up walls for extra storage pieces. Even for the pros, the right layout is often the result of trial and error. "We often start a project by bringing over a roomful of furniture and playing with it to get a realistic sense of how pieces relate," say Todd Nickey and Amy Kehoe. "Floor plans won't tell you you're going to bump your hip on the corner of the dining table."

Custom built-ins can make the most of every nook and cranny. "People often get stuck on the idea that they've absolutely got to have what they think of as a real piece of furniture—a free standing étagère or whatever—even when it's clear it's not going to work," say Andrew Halliday and David Greer. "Built-ins are furniture. We use them to define the space, and as a dramatic way to create more storage." Exploit wall space where floor area is lacking, perhaps by commissioning bookcases that take full advantage of the room's height. If you can't expand out, expand up!

CONSIDER BACKLESS BENCHES
The small, low-ceilinged dining room of Ken Fulk's Provincetown cottage seats twelve thanks to a smart furniture plan: He paired a mix of vintage chairs—originally used in classrooms of the nearby Cape Cod School of Art—with a bench that maximizes seating area and wiggle room, too.

MATH MATTERS

Getting the scale right is essential in a small space, so pick—or customize—perfectly proportioned pieces suited to smaller abodes. Vintage items are often preferable to bulkier contemporary pieces.

DOWNSIZE YOUR SOFA *(right)*

In the living room of their Vermont cottage, Deirdre Heekin and Caleb Barber used a slim settee rather than a full sofa—and pert patent-leather storage cubes versus a space-hogging (and quick-to-get-cluttered) coffee table. A low-profile Barcelona chair has generous proportions that invite lounging yet don't over-whelm the space.

TEENY CAN HAVE BIG PRESENCE *(opposite)*

A pint-sized Smeg fridge brings outsize person-ality to the guest suite of a 1,200-square-foot California beach cot-tage by Krista Ewart. She admits her choice here was stylistic versus functional: "It's not really practical—it's more like a dorm refrigerator."

"Boy, is it cute. It's tiny—perfect for a small kitchen."

—KRISTA EWART

BE ATTENTIVE TO CIRCULATION

Angled or rounded pieces, off-center furniture placement, armless (or low-armed) seating that's easier to shimmy into—these details make a space more physically navigable (and comfortable) while imbuing openness.

ALIGN ALONG THE DIAGONAL *(right)*
To make the salon of a Victorian row house feel larger, designer Barry Dixon arranged French club chairs and a circular ottoman in a diagonal—the longest line in a square room. "It's not a huge room, and we didn't want to block it with a conventional sofa in front of the fireplace. So we threw in a curve, literally, with that round ottoman."

ROUND AND ROUND *(opposite)*
The family room of a Greenwich Village prewar by Fawn Galli features furnishings with minimalist, rounded profiles that make the most of the room's square footage—a pouf, a pebble-shaped coffee table, and a Barbara Barry lounge chair that seems to float on white-lacquered feet.

"I prefer Baroque- and Rococo-style curves and Barbara Barry furniture, which feels French 1940s yet American at the same time. It's graceful and romantic, and the proportions are right for rooms with low ceilings."

—FAWN GALLI

> "People have a tendency to push their furniture up against the walls. But floating the furniture makes a room bigger—even though it doesn't feel like you're maximizing space."
> —TODD NICKEY & AMY KEHOE

ARRANGE FURNITURE TO CREATE A ROOM-WITHIN-A-ROOM

Todd Nickey and Amy Kehoe floated a sofa in the living room of a Venice bungalow. Turning its backside to the front door created a passageway that has the effect of an entry hall in the room.

1. SHAPE TO FIT *(opposite)* Todd Nickey and Amy Kehoe altered a client's walnut dining table to better suit a narrow dining room, tapering one end of the top and replacing the heavy block base with a lighter, airier one. "It was originally rectangular, but the dining room is a throughway, and it didn't allow for an easy flow," they explain. **2. UNMOOR YOUR FURNITURE** It may seem counterintuitive, but pulling pieces away from walls—as Charles O. Schwarz III did for the low-ceilinged living room of an 1830s Greek Revival—aerates close quarters. **3. DINE ON A SETTEE** Mismatched antique chairs lend a relaxed vibe to a dining room by Tom Scheerer. The designer chose a low-armed settee for the far side of the table, making a tight pinch more navigable. **4. THROWING A CURVE** Rounded silhouettes distinguish the living room of Chris Barrett's 1,050-square-foot Spanish Colonial bungalow: 1950s Italian loungers, a midcentury table, and a skirted sofa shaped by sinuous lines. "I used curved furniture that I can easily walk around," the designer notes.

GO THE CUSTOM ROUTE

From bespoke bookcases to drop-down desks, customized built-ins and storage-encompassing furnishings are a savvy solution for eking function out of every square inch.

"People who have these huge houses never see one another. And when they do get together, they usually avoid the great room and sit in the breakfast nook."

—KIM DEMPSTER

SLIP IN STORAGE WHERE YOU CAN
For the dining area of her 1,650-square-foot Marin County beach house, Kim Dempster custom designed a deep seating banquette that accommodates storage underneath and doubles as an extra guest bed in a pinch.

COCOON WITH SHELVES In a New York guest room, Philip Gorrivan framed an upholstered headboard with cerused-oak bookcases. In addition to providing generous storage space, the shelving creates a tailored look—and an enveloping little sleeping spot.

ESTABLISH AN ENTRY A window seat surrounded by built-in bookcases establishes a de facto mudroom in the kitchen of an East Hampton cottage. "You walk right into a bunch of hats and coats and books," says designer Robert Stilin. "It's real life."

DISGUISE UNUSUAL NOOKS *(top)*
In a New York apartment, Alexander Doherty converted an awkwardly shaped master bedroom into a library. Full-height bookcases cleverly mask odd angles while taking advantage of them.

LIFT YOUR CABINETS *(bottom left)*
Summer Thornton maximized storage space in her 105-square-foot Chicago kitchen by extending cabinets all the way to the ceiling, which rises 9-½ feet. "I never understood why everyone doesn't do that. Aside from the practicality, it's also super dramatic—the kitchen Is so small, and the cabinets are so tall." She keeps infrequently used serving pieces on the upper shelves, accessed via step stool.

MOVING ON UP
(bottom right)
A floor-to-ceiling shelving unit forms a vanity in Sara Story's New York dressing room. "I finally got a place to sit and blow-dry my hair and put on my makeup," she says. Daily-use items are kept in drawers; less accessible upper shelves are primarily for display. "The top is for photos and the little things I collect, like bowls, boxes, and perfume bottles."

WORK YOUR WALLS

Even if you're pressed for square footage, you may still have ample wall space that you can put to work. Take advantage of vertical surfaces.

FRAME FAVORITE PIECES WITH BUILT-INS (top) Cerused-oak millwork—from bookcases to bedside tables—features prominently in a New York condo by Andrew Halliday and David Greer. The niche in the den's wall unit was specifically designed for the Peter Hujar photograph and Thai sculpture it houses. "The owner, who was scaling down, asked us to design the apartment like a ship, using every square inch because space is limited," the designer explains.

HANG ART OVER YOUR BOOKS (bottom) Make your vertical surfaces perform double duty by hanging artwork over bookshelves, as Craig Schumacher did in his Dallas living room.

USE BOOKCASES AS DISPLAY VIGNETTES In a Georgetown row house by Mary Douglas Drysdale, vertical space becomes display area. A collection of Limoges and other keepsakes are arranged in ever-changing vignettes on a built-in hutch.

VOILA! INSTANT ROOM

No space for an enclosed foyer, a dedicated dining room, a full office, or a guest suite? Fake it with these clever furniture arrangements and other quick decorative tricks.

Lindsey Bond Meadows hung a shelf for mail and keys near her backdoor entry, creating the function of a foyer and inviting the suggestion of an enclosed room.

Valerie Rice likes using card tables to create a de facto dining room: "You can put a card table wherever," she says. "Use your fine china, and it makes dinner feel luxurious and surprising."

Instant guest room: Myra Hoefer's Sonoma dressing room can host overnighters courtesy of an antique French daybed.

A tucked-away space underneath Melissa Rufty's foyer stairway became a surprisingly serviceable (and sexy) lounge once she added a velvet banquette and a vintage faux-bamboo coffee table. "That's one of my favorite spots in the house. When we have a party, it starts out collecting coats and purses, but it ends up collecting the late-nighters. It's where I hold court."

A full-service home-office zone is hidden behind doors in this multi-tasking kitchen. All that's required are three slim shelves: one for writing and two to stash supplies.

CURTAINED QUARTERS

Use curtains to divide and conquer where solid walls would be too intrusive. Billowing sheers or crisp cotton panels are an effective device for separating spaces without compartmentalizing them—and they're tailor-made for screening storage.

"In a small space, everything should blend...
so it all becomes part of the same gesture."

—SUSAN FERRIER

**NEED A WALL?
TRY A CURTAIN**
"The living room and dining room are really one big room, and it's asymmetrical," says Susan Ferrier of this Alabama townhouse. "On top of that, there was no good wall to put a sofa against. So to fix the asymmetry, I dropped a sheer curtain that runs for 22 feet, and put the sofa against it."

DRAPE YOUR STORAGE *(above)*
Barry Dixon deployed silvery flax curtains to cocoon a bedroom and hide bookcases, reducing visual noise and abetting acoustics while instilling tranquility.

SCREEN WITH SCRIMS *(top right)*
Lindsey Bond Meadows hung a curtain to separate the dining and living areas in her Birmingham, Alabama, home. "They are perfectly proportioned to frame the view out the window." She designed a banquette to improve traffic flow in the pass-through dining room.

MAKE A CANOPY OF CURTAINS *(bottom right)*
Bond Meadows repeated the effect in her small bedroom, where ceiling-hung panels frame the bed to form a casual canopy. The curtains are the same all through the house: "They add softness and height, but they also create order through repetition."

DINING ROOM DO-OVERS

Dining rooms often go underutilized. Converting them to a different function—and carving out an eating nook elsewhere—can be a wonderful space saver. Or preserve your dining room but make it work overtime as a library, office, or media lounge.

> "In small apartments, you need furniture that's multifunctional and can be moved easily."
> —MILES REDD

PUT ALL SURFACES TO WORK WHEN ENTERTAINING (left)
Miles Redd chose a flip-top Chinese Chippendale game table to save space in a Manhattan prewar. "It folds up even smaller, to half its size," says the designer. In addition to the card table, there's a large console that converts to an eight-seater and a round folding table stored in a closet when not in use.

DINING IN (above)
With an eat-in kitchen this vibrant and luxurious, who even needs a dining room? Lindsey Coral Harper furnished the nook with a citrus-y pedestal table and wire side tables that she repurposed into stools. "They're fun, like stool ghosts, you see right through them."

AN INTIMATE EATING ZONE Mica Ertegun placed a 1970s rattan game table in one corner of an artful East Hampton living room, an arrangement that lets the room host meals, too—ensuring activity throughout the day. "My client was emphatic that she wanted to use— to really live in—every single room."

STAIRCASE SPACES

Don't let any corner of your home go unused! One of the most overlooked spots: leftover space above, below, or framed by a staircase.

WHIMSICAL BOOK NOOK

Ann Wolf converted a staircase landing into a children's reading room, hidden behind cheery floor-to-ceiling curtains; a mattress tucked inside the bottom drawer pulls out to host sleepovers. "It's a very private, magical little space at the heart of the house, where your imagination can run wild."

A COZY SPOT FOR MEALS *(above)*
Designer Markham Roberts made clever use of a tight corner in a big kitchen, placing a dining banquette in the odd space above a stairwell. "No one wants to sit in a cavernous space."

INTIMATE CONFINES *(opposite)*
Beside a staircase in a Connecticut Dutch Colonial, Lee Ann Thornton established an intimate bar and seating area. To give the vignette gravitas, she furnished it with a bespoke loveseat and a double-decker coffee table—which offers ample surface space in a small footprint.

ANATOMY OF A HOME

This airy one-bedroom was designed for a 30-something client who frequently entertains. Ashley Whittaker used bold and pretty moves to make a big statement in small confines while still providing ample room to cook, relax, work, and even host cocktail parties.

"Living in a small space is like living on a boat: You need a specific place to store the things you use. And if you don't use them then out they go."

—ASHLEY WHITTAKER

1 BIGGER BUT FEWER "If you have lots of small pieces of furniture in a small room, it can feel cluttered," Whittaker cautions. "Furniture should be scaled to the people who live there—not to the scale of the room. There isn't anything in this apartment that I wouldn't use in a 10,000-square-foot house. Here, there is less furniture, but it's not smaller."

2 BIG LOOKS, SMALL FOOTPRINT To make the chesterfield sofa appear longer, Whittaker ordered a single cushion for the seat. "It's more comfortable than individual cushions—no one falls into the cracks."

3 CLEARLY INSPIRED An acrylic coffee table opens up the main seating area, making it feel less cluttered.

4 PARTY-SAVVY SEATING The Billy Baldwin slipper chair swivels so the sitter can join conversations in other vignettes.

5 **MULTITASK** "Almost all the furniture in the living room is multifunctional. The desk doubles as a buffet and a dining table, the settee pulls up to the desk like a banquette, the bar cart can hold anything—liquor, brunch, desserts." The silver stool, notes Whittaker, "works as a perfect perch. I call it 'the hostess stool'—you can easily pop up and run to the kitchen or move it from group to group."

6 **WORK WHERE YOU EAT** A Parsons table makes an eye-catching display surface—and a hardworking desk. When entertaining, the client uses it as a dining table.

7 **PATTERN PLAY** Osborne & Little's Maharani wallpaper spruces up the entry. "Pattern can actually make a place look larger," says Whittaker. "Some would look at the scale and color of the paper and worry it would be too dark and busy. But the darkness makes the walls recede, and the large pattern gives the room a grander scale. If you used some tiny, all-over pattern on the walls, it would be so low-impact the room would disappear."

"At the end of the day, wallpaper is what makes a place feel finished and decorated. You don't want to repeat the same scale of pattern from one room to another. And you want contrasting colors."

—ASHLEY WHITTAKER

8 **CLEAN SLATE** Whittaker gutted the kitchen, replacing dark cabinetry and terra-cotta tiles with white cupboards and Carrara marble. "The room now feels twice as big." A slim white table provides extra counter space and doubles as a breakfast nook.

9 **EXOTIC TOUCHES** Zebra-print wallpaper and a chinoiserie birdcage lantern inject a dose of whimsy. "When you're working with a small apartment, why not make the kitchen feel like another decorated room?"

10 **SMOOTH TRANSITIONS** Lime-green wallpaper—"a break from all the lavenders and blues"—segues to grasscloth in the bedroom. "You don't want to repeat the same scale of pattern from one room to another," notes Whittaker. "And you want contrasting colors. You can't think about a room on its own. You need to be aware of the room just beyond it, because that's where your eye travels."

KLE PLENTY Antiqued mirror, hand-cut into an emerald shape and inlaid with brass, visually doubles the width of a Manhattan entryway. "The entry is lined with mirrors and the ceiling is silver-leafed to create this dazzling 'wow!' moment—and the illusion of more space," says designer Philip Gorrivan.

FOOLING
THE EYE

"What I love about shiny surfaces
—and that includes mirror—
is that they reflect, which gives
you depth and makes the
room feel larger."
—PHILIP GORRIVAN

You may not be able to get more wiggle room, but you can give rooms the appearance of more square footage through sleight of hand. These designs trick the eye into perceiving more space than is really there, making ceilings seem higher, the distance between walls seem greater, and adjacent spaces seem continuous. The more there is to look at in a room—and the farther your eye travels while taking it all in—the bigger it appears. The strategy is two-pronged: to divert attention from a room's diminutive size, and to draw your gaze to its farthest corners (and beyond).

OPTICAL ILLUSION
David Rockwell used a number of decorative devices to give a cocoon-like media room the impression of more headroom: vertical striped wallpaper (of his own design), a pair of tall shelving units, and window treatments mounted almost to the ceiling. Furthermore, the coffee table's angular shape abets circulation, while its glass top practically disappears.

Mirrors are an especially effective trick, literally doubling your surroundings. Reflective surfaces like lacquer perform the same function, as do mirror-paneled furnishings and gleaming accessories. Transparent finishes do the opposite: Breathe air into a space by making furniture (or whole walls) magically disappear. Accent with pieces made of clear materials like Lucite, which keep rooms looking less cluttered. The same rule applies to opening up views to annex adjacent rooms or patios: Tear down walls, enlarge windows, and swap solid doors for frameless glass. "It's the whole idea of borrowed space," say Andrew Halliday and David Greer.

Sometimes the right move is to reveal; other times, to conceal. Studio apartment dwellers, for instance, may wish to screen a bedroom or kitchen from the main living space—but don't want either area to feel overly cozy or compartmentalized. Cleverly placed furniture like a mid-height bookcase or interior curtains hung floor to ceiling are ideal in these instances. Creating visual blockages encourages you to take in the full sweep of space slowly, suggesting it's more loft-like. "It's all about the reveal, so when you walk in, you don't see everything at once," explains Zach Motl.

MIRROR MANEUVERS

A designer's secret weapon, mirrors can brighten and open up views. There are myriad ways to bounce light around a room, from shimmery lacquered surfaces to mirror-paneled furnishings.

REFLECT AD INFINITUM *(right)*

Shazalynn Cavin-Winfrey designed this bathroom vanity to look like furniture. Floating the unit four inches from the full-height mirrors flanking it helped suggest more spacious confines. The treatment also intensifies the impact of the marble mosaic.

THROUGH THE LOOKING GLASS

(opposite)

Cheetah-print carpeting and a handrail crafted from laurel limbs give Will Merrill's stairwell panache, while his salon-style installation of Tramp Art mirrors provides a lively "look-see" inside the windowless sliver of space.

FAKE A VIEW *(left)*
Gary McBournie high-mounted a giant mirror in the TV room of his Nantucket cottage to create the illusion of a more loft-like environment. "I had the mirror made overscaled. There's only one window in that room, and that mirror becomes a virtual window," he says.

SOFTEN SHINE WITH PATINA *(above)*
In designer Lindsey Bond Meadows's small master bedroom, antiqued glass panels are "a little play on old French trumeau mirrors, the ones large enough to fill the walls of huge houses." A floating desk and Louis Ghost chair keep bulky and leggy furniture to a minimum.

1. THE MORE THE MERRIER Myra Hoefer's Healdsburg living room boasts six looking glasses—two over six feet tall! The tall mirrors double the visual impression of the room and intensify the golden Northern California light. **2. TAKE A SHINE** Tobi Tobin unleashed an arsenal of mirrors, glass transoms and doors, and reflective surfaces to open up the interior of her Hollywood Hills cottage, including this small entryway. Throughout her home, she says, "There are no dead walls without some kind of reflection." **3. DECORATING MAGIC!** In this compact bathroom by Brian J. McCarthy, mirrors framed in polished nickel make the architecture appear to vanish. "It's eight by eight feet. But it looks so huge and feels so light because of all the mirror. It makes the walls disappear, reflecting everything into infinity." **4. MAKE A (BACK)SPLASH** "I thought open shelves would be a great way to display my collections, and I could take the mirrored backsplash up to the ceiling in those spots," says Summer Thornton, describing her 105-square-foot cookery. "The kitchen sparkles. And the mirror also opens it up."

BRING THE OUTDOORS IN A mirrored wall behind an antique bed captures the lush exterior view in a sweet sleeping chamber by Mimi McMakin. To further the indoor/outdoor connection, McMakin swathed the room in matching Brunschwig & Fils Bengali wallpaper and fabric. "The birds and vines make you feel as if you're sleeping outside."

ILLUSIONS OF GRANDEUR

Hanging artwork to mimic a view is a savvy move in window-challenged rooms. It's all about optical illusions.

"Bold, graphic gestures look cool in small spaces."

—RICHARD BORIES & JAMES SHEARRON

DAZZLE (AND DISTRACT) WITH FINE ART

In his 350-square-foot studio, Matthew Bees hung framed academic drawings on all the walls, even on the room divider that screens his sleeping area. The wraparound treatment disguises the fact that it's a partition, making it read like a solid wall. Furnishings are smartly chosen for a small space: an armless settee, a small pedestal table, and a pair of stools/side tables that can be moved around as needed.

NO WHITE-BOX GALLERY Richard Bories and James Shearron designed a 900-square-foot Chicago one-bedroom as a calm backdrop for rotating art. "First we made the background seamless, like gallery walls: We got rid of all the trim and moldings," says the duo. "Essentially, we made the living room and bedroom into flat gray boxes so the client can move around his art as much as he wants. It looks good everywhere."

TRANSPARENT SOLUTIONS

Furnishings made of Lucite, Plexiglas, glass, and even wire disappear from view—creating a lighter, less-cluttered look that puts the emphasis on other decorative features.

GETTING THE HANG OF IT *(above)*
Heather Moore hung a playful Plexiglas ball chair to lend a gossamer feeling to a teenage girl's bedroom. Reinforcing the illusion of loftiness are a metallic silver ceiling, a wide-striped carpet, and an oversize upholstered headboard that stretches luxuriously high.

CLEARLY CHIC *(opposite)*
Hillary Thomas and Jeff Lincoln referenced William Haines signatures—a game table and tufted chairs—to instill a "sophisticated salon" feeling in a Washington, D.C., town house. "The Lucite-base game table has an open look, so the room doesn't feel too clogged," the duo explains.

PRECIOUS OBJECTS
In a New York apartment, Philip Gorrivan chose a glass tabletop for a jewelry-like base. "A solid table would have felt like an obstruction," he says. "I also designed furniture that can seat the maximum number of people, like the banquette. They hug the walls, and that makes the space feel bigger."

THINGS ARE LOOKING UP

Hanging curtains floor to ceiling creates an elongated line that makes windows—and thus rooms—appear taller. Matchstick blinds hung just above the windows complete the effect.

Gary McBournie used the same window treatments—high-mounted matchstick blinds paired with elegant curtains—throughout his 1828 Nantucket cottage. "Somehow the space feels bigger if it's unified. The curtains are hung as high as possible for that same reason."

Myra Hoefer was influenced by the French interior design tradition of hanging window treatments—as well as paintings, mirrors, and sconces—high on the walls, rendering her low ceilings more loft-like.

Columnar curtains and high-mounted drapery rods draw the eye up in an eaved master bedroom by Kevin Isbell.

Hillary Thomas and Jeff Lincoln decked out the entryway of a New York town house with striped wallpaper. A boldly patterned floor bolsters the graphic punch, as does a white Roman shade bordered in crisp black.

In her 650-square-foot Manhattan studio, Maureen Footer hung draperies, a wall tapestry, and a foot-deep bed canopy right below the molding to draw attention to the ceiling plane, enhancing the sense of spaciousness.

STRETCH SPACE

Stripes in any direction create visual movement with the suggestion of more space around the corner or ceiling to floor.

LINING UP (*right*)
"Stripes are a nice, graphic design element that can bring movement and pattern to a room, but not in a busy way," says Angela Free, who used two tones of tile to embolden a 37-square-foot bathroom. "As soon as the tiles went up—whoosh! The room opened up. The fact that they wrap the entire room creates flow, a borderless space."

VERDANT VERTICALS (*opposite*)
Frank de Biasi treated the living room of a Miami guesthouse to bold green-striped walls.

"Vertical stripes are fun, and they also lift the low ceiling."

—FRANK DE BIASI

"In the living and dining rooms—which is really one big room—
I refinished the wood floors, and instead of using heavy rugs,
I painted a pattern of thick and narrow stripes over the stained
floor. It jazzes everything up."

—BILL INGRAM

STRIPES UNDERFOOT (*above*)
All is crisp in Bill Ingram's 1,400-square-foot Birmingham, Alabama, cottage. In the house's main space, the architect painted stripes on the floor to add pizzazz, open up cramped rooms, and wake up Colonial style.

LINEAR MOVEMENT (*opposite*)
Stripy Linac marble marches across the floor, over the tub, and up the wall, giving this master bath graphic punch. "The stone, the 12-foot ceilings, and the focal point of the water altar emphasize the linear quality of the room, so it feels much larger than you would expect," say Sarah Luhtala and David Katz. The shower curtain hangs from a recessed ceiling track to eliminate the visual intrusion of a rod, allowing an uninterrupted flow of striations.

COMMODIOUS KITCHENS

An open kitchen can maximize usable space; don't be afraid of tearing down a wall to connect an adjacent room. Appliances can always be hidden.

"You make a lot of sacrifices living in a small space, but style does not have to be one of them."

—NICK OLSEN

USE APPLIANCES AS UNEXPECTED DISPLAY SPACE

Nick Olsen covered a client's fridge with a grid of Polaroids, mounted with double-sided foam tape, to create a mini art gallery in the 295-square-foot studio. "The refrigerator is this big, hulking thing in the room. You have to jazz it up, because there's no getting around it."

HIDE A KITCHEN IN PLAIN SIGHT *(above and left)*
The main space of Bill Ingram's 1,400-square-foot Birmingham, Alabama, cottage combines living, dining, and cooking areas. "I managed to fit a small kitchen in the far end of the living-dining room. The counter and oak cabinets are one big built-in piece that I designed to look like an English campaign chest. The countertops are low, so you don't see them from the living areas."

EXPANDING BATHROOMS

Full-height glass-enclosed showers with continuous flooring—running straight into the wet area—make tiny bathrooms appear larger, keeping the space open and visually cohesive.

DOUBLE GLAZED
Throughout Mark Egerstrom's 1,200-square-foot West Hollywood house, rooms encased in glass feel as big as the outdoors. The master bath shower, for instance, opens to a private deck via full-height sliding doors. "Your sight line goes to the windows and the space outside, which makes the room seem much larger," he says.

ALL THE RIGHT ANGLES
In a New York bathroom by Alla Akimova, a chevron-patterned floor, composed of Dark Emperador and Thassos marble, runs straight into the shower stall. "If I had changed materials, it would have interrupted the space," she notes. Walls are reflective crystallized glass.

A PORTAL BETWEEN ROOMS *(above and right)* Inspired by diamond-shaped windows in stately old Syracuse houses, Thom Filicia introduced several in his own abode—including one that punctuates a screen wall between the master suite's sleeping and bathing areas.

ANATOMY OF A HOME

Designer Kelly Kilsen conjured a romantic past inside her no-frills one-bedroom apartment by deploying architectural salvage—including windows and doors—and adding elegant moldings, sparkling mirror, and a fresh blue-and-white palette.

"People think, 'Small space, why bother?' But I say, 'Amp it up! Don't skimp!' The less room you have, the more you appreciate über-luxury."

—KELLY GIESEN

1 TAKE A SHINE TO MIRRORS "I'm a huge fan of glass and mirrors, which expand the space, reflect light, and bring views inside," says Giesen. Here, she used reflective elements aplenty: mirrored French doors, kitchen cabinets, and doorknob plates; metallic wallpaper and textiles; crystal chandeliers.

2 LOOK UP—AND OUT Giesen played up the room's loft-like proportions. "Chandeliers draw your eye upward. The French doors stand nine feet tall. My living room curtains go all the way to the ceiling." The latter's large, graphic pattern also calls attention to the oversize window, and thus the view—another space-enlarging trick.

3 CHOOSE UNOBTRUSIVE FURNISHINGS "All the seating is low. Chairs are off the floor on exposed legs, and the coffee table is made of there-but-not-there Lucite," says Giesen. "These pieces keep the space from feeling crowded."

4 **SEE THE LIGHT** Removing one wall transformed what had been a dark galley into an airy eat-in kitchen. A pair of mirrored cupboards are flanked by glass-door cupboards with mirrored backs.

5 **THROWING A CURVE** "Because the front door is right in the kitchen, this had to be a fantastic space," the designer notes. "There was a weird window that was too high to see out of, and I considered blocking it off. But that's the first thing guests face coming in, so I decided to turn it into a dramatic feature by building an oval inside the rectangular frame and uplighting it at night."

6 **UNCLUTTER THE KITCHEN** All the appliances are under the counter with matching fronts, to keep a clean, open feel. The microwave is hidden behind mirrored doors above the sink.

7 **FAKE A FOYER** To give presence to a standard entry door and separate it from the kitchen, Giesen created a "foyer" by framing the door with closets and a transom all dressed up with mirrors and molding. "The moldings, cabinetwork, and floors are all new, but I detailed them to look as if they'd been here a hundred years."

8 **POCKET DOORS SAVE SPACE** A mirrored sliding door shields the bathroom, which features a Venetian etched mirror and shimmery mosaic.

9 **CLOSET CASE** "It's important to use every inch you can for storage. I stash office stuff inside the paneled closets on either side of the front door. Transoms up top hide items I rarely use, like Christmas lights. Since you can see into every room—the bath opens into the kitchen!—I don't want anything that looks like clutter."

10 **SPARKLE PLENTY** Shimmer continues in the bedroom, clad in John Mahoney's Kiku Komon wallpaper, printed on Mylar. Giesen hung the silver-upholstered headboard on the wall to save floor space. Curtains on either side of the window seat conceal built-in bookcases.

LAST WORDS

When it comes to creating magic, these designers know it's all done with mirrors.

"A mirror makes a fabulous backdrop for art. I love to prop a painting in front, or hang it right on top."

—ROBERT BROWN

"I mirrored the ceiling of a powder room and put a small modern crystal chandelier in the center to obscure the mirror. The room is like a jewel box, with the light appearing to float above."

—THOMAS PHEASANT

"Mirror the reveals of any window: It will feel like a bay window."

—ERIC COHLER

"I'll put an upholstered bench or console against a mirrored wall. It seems to double in size, and so does the room. The idea is to pretend the mirror isn't there, so you want it to be as big as possible. Then it becomes a doorway into another space."

—BENJAMIN NORIEGA-ORTIZ

"I find them so glamorous, and they're a great way to expand a space. A mirrored screen can transform a room from drab to fabulous in an instant. Attached to one side of a nook, it creates a door: Voila! Hidden storage for linens, luggage, even a TV."

—NANCY CORZINE

"In an entry, I mounted antiqued mirror on all four walls. It glowed like a lightbox."

—CAREY MALONEY

"I love putting mirrors in built-in cabinetry. I have mirrored glass in the pilasters separating the bays of books in my library/dining room, and the effect at night during a dinner party is incredible. The mirrors reflect the shimmering light of the chandelier, bouncing it all around the room."

—JONATHAN BERGER

"In my apartment, I used a very large mirror to exaggerate the size of my dining area. The larger the mirror, the larger the impact. Just be sure it's opposite something you don't mind seeing two of!"

—MARIETTE HIMES GOMEZ

HIGH STYLE, HIGH SHINE Miles Redd lacquered the living area of a dark two-bedroom Manhattan apartment in Farrow & Ball's Hague Blue. "My solution was to make every single surface count, especially the reflective ones," says the designer. Lacquered walls, he notes, "are a great way to do a moody color because of the way it reflects light. It doesn't look dark so much as rich."

COLOR
CONSCIOUS

"In a small space, I like to take
one strong color
and use it everywhere."

—MILES REDD

esign advice for small spaces can seem counterintuitive, and color is no exception. Conventional wisdom is incongruous: "Go white!" "Go dark!" "Avoid extremes!" Every strategy is valid and has its place; the key is knowing what will work for your particular situation. The following pages demonstrate the full tonal spectrum, from white-on-white to all black and everything in between, and explain why each choice is effective in its context.

Strategic use of color palettes—via paint in particular—can create the illusion of greater space or, in contrast, heighten the coziness. In essence, you can either mitigate smallness or celebrate it. A pale, restful hue, applied to everything from walls to flooring to upholstery, creates a spare backdrop, which optically enlarges a room. Dark hues, conversely, embrace you and confer intimacy.

Color isn't just about the shade; pattern and even finish also play a big part in how it affects your perception of space. A lacquer or high-gloss on walls or furnishings offers a slick shine that imparts expansiveness. A light-absorbing matte finish, however, recedes from view, so that you sense a room's volume and not its barriers. If you go dark in compact quarters, go glossy, too, so that the walls seem to fade away instead of close in.

With paint, you'll also have to consider whether to treat walls and trims the same color, not to mention the ceiling. Whether you choose a light or dark scheme—or a happy medium—many designers encourage carrying it seamlessly through a space, continuity being a shortcut to spaciousness. Barry Dixon advocates a completely monochrome scheme: "Use one color on every door, every ceiling, the trim, the window frames, and the door frames, as if you're dipping the whole room in a bucket of paint. It takes away all the boundaries and you're left with the infinity of the universe. It's like Houdini came in and decorated." Who doesn't want a little magic in their home—no matter the size (or color)?

A BLUE MOOD
A custom lapis hue creates "moody drama" in the low-ceilinged breakfast room of an 1830s Greek Revival. "At night, my clients host intimate dinners there," says designer Charles O. Schwarz III. "It's really romantic with the candles flickering against the dark blue."

LIGHT AND BRIGHT

Ethereal hues imbue tranquility and calm. A coat of white paint is like a breath of fresh air, giving formerly dark and cramped quarters an inner glow.

TASTEFUL HUES
Mimi McMakin chose a vanilla-and-lime palette for a Palm Beach mai-sonette, making it feel much larger than its 640 square feet. "These are soothing, easy, tropical colors that everybody loves."

THE MILKY WAY *(above)*
Creamy tones prevail in Peter Frank's Hudson, New York, dining room—and serve as a sedate backdrop to an eclectic mix of furniture and objects. Walls are Pudding Mold by Sherwin-Williams; the floor is Farrow & Ball's Off-White.

ADD WHITE SPACE *(top right)*
Stephen Shubel whitewashed his Sausalito cottage to instill a light and lively ambience. "The walls and ceilings were originally dark redwood, and the floors were oak. It was very claustrophobic," he describes. "The first thing I did was paint everything white to open it up and make it feel better." Moreover, he says, the spare backdrop draws attention to the sculptural forms of the furnishings, an assemblage of French antiques.

LIGHTEN UP DARK ROOMS *(bottom right)*
Bill Ingram doused a small guest room in mellow hues. "This spare bedroom is the tiniest, darkest room in the house, so I gave it a touch of color. The bedding adds lime green, and these watercolors of cathedrals have amazing details."

COLOR DYNAMICS

Done with purpose and flair, color-saturated rooms have a jewel-box vibe. Paint every surface the same hue to create cohesion and intensify the drama.

COCOON WITH COLOR (*opposite*)
David Kaihoi chose Benjamin Moore's Purple Haze for the living area of his 390-square-foot one-bedroom. "There's a density of color here that makes it enveloping and warm instead of pinched and anemic. It sort of wraps around you," he says. "We found that a small white box tends to look more cluttered when you have things."

BOLD MOVES (*above*)
A few feet away in his kitchen, Kaihoi dipped cabinets in glossy Bottle Green by Fine Paints of Europe to reflect light and make the room feel larger. "I wanted it to be a gutsy one-note accent to all the color, pattern, and objects in the rest of the apartment. I did it in high gloss because it has a more luxe look than flat paint. It has that reflective, glassy quality that can light up and expand a small room."

IN THE SWIM OF IT
"In my little library, I painted every square inch—except the ceiling—Benjamin Moore's Ash Blue in high gloss to make it shine," designer Kate Coughlin says of her Boston home. "When I first saw it, I felt as if I were in an aquarium, but now it's one of my favorite rooms!"

"You can paint small spaces dark colors. Deep tones absorb the light, decreasing shadows so that the space appears seamless and therefore larger. A dark color on the ceiling makes it recede into the night."

—FRANCES SCHULTZ

SLEEP TIGHT
In the 9-by-12-foot bedroom of Frances Schultz's beach cottage, a coat of dark paint counteracts the closing-in effect of low 7-foot ceilings. "I chose a deep, glossy, turquoise-y blue to envelop the bedroom, ceiling included. It looks like an ocean—waves and all—thanks to bumpy old stucco walls."

1. **SPRING FOR GREEN** A white canopy bed seems to float within verdant surroundings. Liza Gusler painted the wall paneling and trim the same hue for uniformity and to make the ceiling look higher. "The color is a great mood enhancer; chlorophyll for the spirit!" **2. GO DEEP** Instead of fighting the darkness in this small entry hall, Daniel Sachs played it up with a sultry azure hue: Benjamin Moore's moody Knoxville Gray. **3. DARK AND DRAMATIC** Stephen Shubel's black-painted bedroom is a moody contrast to his otherwise all-white cottage. "You have to be careful with black, just like you have to be careful with gold leaf," he cautions. "It can look cheap and sleazy." Here, he tempered inky hues with white floors and accents. Genuine Fake Books wallpaper by Deborah Bowness creates the illusion of more space. **4. CREATE A WOW! MOMENT** Paint a closet a glossy color, hang a mirror and sconces, add a vanity, and voilà: a glamorous little dressing room! Designer Mary McDonald says "I address walk-in closets as sanctuaries. I love to create small niches, and a place to sit while you get ready for the day or night."

IN THE RED

Philip Gorrivan deployed luscious color and gleaming surfaces to turn a 1,200-square-foot city apartment into an alluring jewel box. Walls are lacquered in a custom red from Fine Paints of Europe: "We used nine layers of Hollandlac paint, which is basically like marine enamel," he explains.

GO BOLD

Be strategic with color.

"I prefer dark walls in bedrooms. I don't mind a bedroom that feels small, since it's primarily used for sleeping—a kind of sanctuary."
—MOISES ESQUENAZI

"Using brighter colors opens a small room up. Since I love bright colors and wacky patterns, my compromise in small spaces is a linear pattern in vivid colors."
—LESLIE KLOTZ

"If a room is already dark and small, make it darker and smaller! Then it feels deliberately intimate."
—ERINN VALENCICH

"I like a darker color because it creates shadows in the corners, a sense of mystery."
—THOMAS JAYNE

"I always like dark color in a small room because it makes it look bigger."
—MARIO BUATTA

"Create contrast with color. Stain the floor dark, use light colors on walls, and paint the ceiling a lighter white. This helps the eye travel up the walls, giving a sense of more space."
—MAXWELL GILLINGHAM-RYAN

"I believe a rich, dark color actually makes the walls recede, giving the illusion of a larger space."
—CARRIE FUNDINGSLAND

A VERTICAL OFFICE Deirdre Heekin and Caleb Barber gave over one wall of their bedroom to a small home office—using just a slim console, comfy accent chair, and pin board that take up little room but add major function.

DEFINE SPACE WITH COLOR

Bold hues applied selectively can add architectural interest without overwhelming small rooms. Use fields or blocks of color to define distinct zones within open-plan spaces or to punctuate a neutral backdrop.

MELLOW YELLOW
Mary Douglas Drysdale helped her clients—an empty-nest couple—downsize from a five-bedroom to a 500-square-foot row house. A single narrow room serves as a living area, dining area, and a workspace, with zones established by the Madeline Weinrib rug. "The strength of the rug's color grounds and ties together the seating area," she says. "It also defines a little space at the front door for a foyer and, on the other side, allows for a non-carpeted area for the dining table."

PAINT A FAUX HEADBOARD In the bedroom of their Vermont cottage, Deirdre Heekin and Caleb Barber created the effect of a headboard with a crisp square of Benjamin Moore's Iron Mountain. "We love dark, saturated colors, given that so much of our year is spent in winter light. They're warm and enveloping."

REFINE SPACES WITH A FINE FINISH

Lacquer, burnished-to-a-shine, Venetian plaster and other special finishes can give rooms a lit-from-within glow.

USE TEXTURE TO BRING DIMENSION TO A ROOM (right) Chris Barrett resurfaced the interior of her 1,050-square-foot bungalow with integrally colored plaster. "It really gives the walls depth, which makes the spaces look larger." Especially in a milky tone, she says: "My color scheme is white on white on white, along with the natural colors of wood, leather, and textiles."

OVERHEAD SHINE (opposite) In this modestly sized Chicago bedroom, Richard Bories and James Shearron juxtaposed pale gray walls with a shimmery ceiling, painted Farrow & Ball's high-gloss Hague Blue. "In small, modern apartments you have to create dramatic moments that offset the lack of detail—but don't hog space. So we lacquered the bedroom ceiling this fabulous dark blue that's almost black, like the midnight sky."

UNUSUAL COLORS (right)
Mustard Olive by Benjamin Moore sets aglow Bill Brockschmidt's 640-square-foot Manhattan apartment, a double-height studio with a sleeping loft. "It's a great backdrop for art, it's a color that works in winter and summer, and it's not so refined that it's off-putting. It's a very relaxing color to live with." He even dyed the curtains to match the walls: "It would be too chopped up with a contrasting color."

A REFRESHING COCKTAIL OF COLOR (opposite)
Miles Redd drenched his NoHo kitchen in Bamboo Leaf 103A from Fine Paints of Europe. "There's something refreshing about emerald green. It puts a modern spin on a tiny Manhattan kitchen and feels cool and sparkling, especially in this glassy finish. Kind of like a gin and tonic."

ANATOMY OF A HOME

Debunking the myth that a light color is the best strategy for visually enlarging small abodes, husband-wife design duo Philip Cozzi and Kristin Hein lacquered the interior of their petite Cape Cod cottage in a dark black-green paint. The deep, aqueous hue is mysterious and inviting.

"At night, the dark walls dissolve so there's no differentiation between interior and exterior."
—KRISTIN HEIN

1 A WET SHINE Kristin Hein and Philip Cozzi had Fine Paints of Europe match a favorite green in lacquer-like gloss to reflect the bay's shimmer and depth. "It's sort of recreating the essential experience of being in or on the water," says Hein. "Sometimes at night, the walls look like they're going on and on because the reflections keep continuing. The reflectivity was important to us, because of the view. We wanted a lacquer finish like you'd get on a boat. Everything is set off by the backdrop of high gloss."

2 MAXIMIZE SEATING Built-in banquettes evoke a snug ship cabin in the living area. "We can seat about 15 if we pile them in and they sit on the banquettes and all the various stools and chairs," says Hein. "The trick is to move things around while taking advantage of every nook and cranny."

3 **EMBRACE THE KITCHEN** The front door opens directly into the galley kitchen, an integral part of the living room. Treating it to the same hue and illuminating it with a chandelier made it less obtrusive.

4 **GO BELOW THE ISLAND** "We have only X amount of space, so the kitchen has to exist right where it is. But the last thing we wanted to see was a refrigerator," says Cozzi.

⑤ DO THE SLIDE In the 28-inch-wide hall shoehorned behind the chimney, pocket doors save precious space. Use sliders where possible in place of swinging doors.

⑥ REPEAT COLOR FOR CONTINUITY Subway tiles carry the sea green palette into the shipshape bathroom.

⑦ SHIMMER TIMES TWO A French gilt floor mirror expands the bedroom, adding to the reflectivity of the walls and ceiling. "The bedroom is like a dream machine," enthuses Cozzi. "You wake up incredibly rested."

PRINTS CHARMING David Netto used Josef Frank's Hawaii fabric to fashion a headboard in a Long Island bedroom. "It creates a little world within the bed alcove," the designer says. "Guests feel like they're sleeping in an enchanted garden."

THE JEWEL-BOX EFFECT

"In a small space you view things close at hand, so in many ways the detail is more important than it might be in a grander space."

—MARSHALL WATSON
& JEFFREY KILMER

The previous chapters demonstrate how to make petite quarters look and feel bigger—largely by downplaying their smallness. For many though, "small" is not a problem to be solved but a positive attribute to be played up and, indeed, celebrated. There's a reason we inevitably gravitate to the teensiest room in the house, whether a breakfast nook or a gem-like bedroom slipped under the eaves: Small is synonymous with charming and cozy. Intimately proportioned spaces are perfect places to enjoy alone time or intimacy. Snug seating, for instance, can make any meal more romantic or a gathering more festive. Many of us need the enveloping comfort of a little nest to retreat from the world to recharge. "I think we all gravitate to cozy spaces," says Mimi McMakin. "We're happiest in our bathtubs!"

The following projects embrace and exploit the joys of small-space living rather than apologizing for its challenges. Small quarters give a humanistic scale to any home. And, decoratively speaking, they perfect places for luxurious touches that are best appreciated up close. (Which accounts for designers' fondness for tricking out tiny powder rooms in opulent finishes and dazzling wallpapers!) Restraint may be the secret behind many space-enhancing tricks, but not in these jewel boxes, where indulgence is the name of the game. "In a small space, you want every room to feel like a destination," says Philip Gorrivan. Here's how.

BIG MOVES IN SMALL SPACES

A little room is the perfect location to indulge in dazzling accents or superluxe materials that are best appreciated up close—and that might be budget busters elsewhere: cane-covered walls, op-art wallpaper, sumptuous fabrics.

A SCENIC VIEW
In a Manhattan apartment, a small master bedroom has walls upholstered in Quadrille's Cholet, a neo-classical toile so richly dense with images that "it just becomes texture," says designer Michael Formica.

1. **WELCOME TO THE JUNGLE** Steven Sclaroff clad the walls and door of a TriBeCa loft's tiny vestibule in Hinson's banana-leaf print. "It's great to plaster claustrophobic, windowless spaces with pattern. I love the offbeat context and the goofy theatricality of these enormous banana leaves: There's also the joke of having something so about the outdoors and nature in this hopelessly interior closet of a room." 2. **WEAVING IN LUXURY** The sectional sofa in this library is big enough for the whole family to pile on and watch TV—but the room itself is quite intimately proportioned. Tom Samet took advantage of that feature, dressing the walls in caning by Fabrizi Furniture. 3. **RAISING THE BAR** Doubling as a bar during parties, a butler's pantry by Gary McBournie is outfitted with fabric-skirted cabinets and hand-painted walls. 4. **INTO THE WOODS** British artist Richard Woods was commissioned to work his faux-bois magic on this bar, transforming a closet-like space into a vivid focal point. "It's whimsical, fun, and unexpected," says designer Mica Ertegun.

THE MAGIC OF MORE

Conventional wisdom suggests paring back in small quarters, but these spaces revel in the joy of abundance.

"I don't think you should restrain yourself! Big, bright, and bold actually makes small spaces seem larger."

—KRISTA EWART

EMBRACE MAXIMALISM (left) Krista Ewart didn't shy from outfitting this California beach cottage with abundant patterns, furnishings, and objects. "The more statement pieces, the better. I'm all for lots of accessories—they keep your eye moving around. You don't even have time to notice the size of the room."

TANTALIZE THE EYE (opposite) Chris Barrett built full-height shelving in the dining area of her 1,050-square-foot Hollywood home. "It actually feels bigger now that I put the bookcases in," she says. "The walls don't close in on you, because there are so many things to look at on the shelves." Barrett offers advice for keeping compositions clean, not cluttered: "Don't fill every space. You need to leave space around things that are grouped."

GO FOR THE BOLD

Exuberant patters, luscious hues, and precious materials offer major graphic impact—and let small rooms dream big.

ENLIGHTEN WITH METALLICS

Benjamin Dhong gave this dining room a sumptuous backdrop with gilded wallpaper. "This is a classic San Francisco row house—the dining room is basically a hallway between the kitchen and living room, and it doesn't get a lot of sun," he says. "The gilded wallpaper reflects a lot of light, making the room come alive."

"It's one of my own designs, inspired by a painted ceiling I saw in Italy. I love that kind of exotic, almost Middle Eastern pattern."

—SHEILA BRIDGES

DRESS UP KITCHENS IN PATTERNED WALLPAPER *(above, left)*
Her Manhattan kitchen may be on the small side, but Sheila Bridges didn't let that cramp her style. "It's always a challenge to come up with something that's going to be exciting in a small space, and that wallpaper is unexpected. There's nothing over the top about my kitchen, and the metallic wallpaper adds a little glamour."

AN EXOTIC COLLAGE *(above, right)*
An exuberant mix of worldly patterns gives a small space major presence. "It was difficult, almost like doing boat design," says Daniel Sachs of the cramped girl's bedroom, in which he needed to fit a bed, a closet, a desk, and a chair.

COLOR RIOT
Color and pattern collide to energize Anthony Baratta's Miami living room, spiced up with orange walls, curvaceous furniture, and a spiraling rug. "I wanted a color scheme different from any I'd used before, so I chose orange, yellow, and white—nothing black."

WINNER LOOS

Give powder rooms pow! Miniscule rooms are the perfect spot to indulge in busy patterns and unusual imagery on the walls.

WATER'S EDGE

Mona Ross Berman enlivened a loo with vibrant turquoise wallpaper. "I use color sparingly, but I like to go all out in smaller spaces like powder rooms and mudrooms; they're places where you can gild the lily. We used a loud geometric print in a bright ocean blue to give this room a slightly over-the-top feeling."

1. PERFECT PLUMMAGE Florence Broadhurst's peacock-feather print dresses up a Park Avenue apartment by Christina Murphy. The designer even carried the pattern to the guest-towel embroidery. **2. INTO THE WOODS** Ashley Whittaker chose ersatz trees for this WC: Cole & Son's Woods wallcovering from Lee Jofa. The motif's linear quality pulls the eye up, making the room seem loftier,while the angles of the branches keep the small space from feeling too boxy. **3. PRINTS CHARMING** A Pierre Frey ikat gives a slim powder room by Alex Hitz an exotic edge. The vertical orientation of the pattern, meanwhile, creates the impression of greater ceiling height—an effect intensified by the tall, narrow proportions of the mirror frame. **4. FLOWER POWER** For the powder room of a Greenwich Village prewar, Fawn Galli had the mirror painted to match the floral-print wallpaper, Cole & Son's Orchid. The dynamism of the pattern injects movement in the snug confines.

ONE-ROOM WONDERS

Check out these studios, lofts, and hard-working living spaces, which artfully combine multiple functions. They're also models of smart zoning, with furniture plans that establish areas for different uses.

"Various focal points draw the eye to the edges of the room, making the space look larger."

—PETER DUNHAM

LIVING LARGE

Peter Dunham's client wanted this room to play four roles: lounge, library, dining area, and home office. The designer delivered with a desk tucked in one corner, a round table that does triple duty, and a fluid furniture plan that allows for spur-of-the-moment repositioning. "The seating is arranged for conversation and the skirted dining table doubles as a place for books and a buffet."

A MODEL OF MULTITASKING

Zach Motl's studio apartment is a case study in space efficiency. "It's about how you arrange furniture, and how the pieces play off one another. The bed is in its own little niche; I call that the bedroom. The office is where my desk is, and the desk is opposite the bed. The books are in another corner—you could say that's the library."

EXHIBITION HALL(WAYS)

What hallways lack in square feet they often make up for in under utilized wall space—a gallery for art or a room with new purpose.

TURN A CORRIDOR INTO A ROOM
John Saladino used stone columns and taffeta portieres to break up a long hallway, giving it a feeling of ceremony.

1. **SENSE OF PLACE** In the salonlike entry hall of her New York studio, Ellen O'Neill clustered black and white sketches on one wall. "It makes the hallways feel like a 'place' and not just a thoroughfare." 2. **VANITY FAIR** In the same house, Markham reimagined the hallway leading to the master bath as a dressing room with a vanity. A large mirror, ice-crystal sconces, and Lucite pulls enhance the light-and-airy vibe. 3. **A DOSE OF GLAMOUR** High-gloss black wallpaper reflects an antique runner and a cane étagère in an art-lined hallway leading to Stan Topol's Atlanta office. 4. **GROUP THERAPY** In a skylit hall, black-and-white photos are crowded for intimacy. Throughout the house, says Bonnie Edelman, "we sacrificed wall space for windows, and we have a great collection of photos and art. The only way to display them was salon-style hangings, floor to ceiling. It creates an inviting and interactive space where anyone who walks by can get stuck, reminiscing."

SNUG AS A BUG

Canopy beds, bunk beds, window seats, little nooks—everyone inevitably gravitates to these cozy cocoons. Sheers and curtains help establish the room-within-a-room vibe.

"There's something magical about being in a small space. You don't feel lonely. Energy can only go so far."

—KIM DEMPSTER

SLEEPS SIX IN A PINCH
Lined with six bunks, a bedroom in Kim Dempster's beach cottage recalls a ship's cabin. "Kids just love that room, and they'll hang out down there even when it's not bedtime," the designer explains. "You have your own little compartment, and you can get in and close the curtains. You can have the most intimate conversations in a small space—and the best sleep in a cozy little bedroom."

THE OVERNIGHTERS (left)
A bedroom for three sleeps twelve during slumber parties thanks to built-in bunk beds. "Their friends are always spending the night," explains Sally Markham. "Kids love small, protective environments—think fort pillows and pup tents. More than just comforting, they're loads of fun."

YACHT-LIKE EFFICIENCY (below)
In the guest room of designer Stephen Shubel's Sausalito cottage, shipshape striped curtains frame an alcoved sleeping spot with built-in drawers: "It's supposed to look like a berth on a boat," he says.

BEDS TO IMPRESS

Hideaway Murphy beds may have their place, but some designers advocate flaunting a bed right out in the open. Just make it worthy of the square footage it hogs—think upholstered headboards, flouncy bedskirts, and monogrammed sheets.

CELEBRATE THE BED!
Nick Olsen showcased the sleeping area of a client's 295-square-foot Brooklyn studio. "I suppose [Murphy beds] are convenient, but I find them slightly depressing," he admits. "I'd prefer to be comfortable on a real bed."

"A bed should be accessible, and it should be inviting."

—MAUREEN FOOTER

SHOWING OFF
Maureen Footer's bed holds court in one corner of her 650-square-foot Manhattan studio. "If you're going to go for it, you might as well go all the way—drape it, curtain it, hang paintings in the canopy, and make a statement out of it," she says.

TURN ANGLES INTO OPPORTUNITIES

Large houses have little rooms and neglected spaces. Turn any challenging configurations into a triumph of ingenuity—and intimacy.

CLOSET CASE
Gary McBournie converted a master suite's walk-in closet into a small dressing room, using the same wall treatment in both spaces for continuity. "The closet becomes a room of its own. It's really cozy in there."

PUT YOUR ATTIC TO WORK *(above)*
Ken Fulk carved out a home office in his 1850s Provincetown abode by shoehorning it into a nook beneath the top-floor eaves. Built-in cabinets make efficient use of space in the angular aerie.

TAKE A SHINE *(opposite)*
Katie and Jason Maine clad a loft bedroom in op-art custom wallpaper from Brunschwig & Fils. "It would have been a sad little attic-like space if we didn't make an effort to turn it into a super-groovy teenage girl's room," they explain. "To make it seem bright, we added skylights and printed the wallpaper on reflective Mylar."

ANATOMY OF A HOME

Designer Bill Brockschmidt shares his New York mini-loft with partner Richard Dragisic. The space fits its owners like a glove courtesy of custom built-ins, including a secretary-style drop-leaf desk, a cozy sleeping alcove, and a staircase that incorporates storage. There's a place for everything—even a harpsichord.

"Minimalism is very difficult to do well in a small space. You have to maintain things more rigorously. But if you forget to put a sweater away or your shoes are on the floor, they don't look out of place." —BILL BROCKSCHMIDT

1 DOUBLE DUTY In the dining-library area of the main living space, a staircase leading to the sleeping loft incorporates bookshelves. The landing doubles as a sideboard and bar when Brockschmidt entertains. "All the glasses get stacked on the lower steps. Of course, that means we quite literally can't go to bed till we clean up."

2 USE ART TO DISTRACT AND DISGUISE Artworks are hung salon-style on walls painted Mustard Olive by Benjamin Moore. The arrangement continues right over closet doors that open to reveal the television. "We were influenced by the London home of neoclassical architect Sir John Soane," the designer continues. "Every space is covered with something beautiful and interesting."

3 DON'T REVEAL THE WHOLE SPACE AT ONCE "Some apartments are dead ends. Here you spiral into the living room and then you turn around and see the dining room. The spiraling effect makes the apartment feel gracious."

4 BESPOKE BUILT-INS
The bookcase near the kitchen incorporates a pull-down desk, drawers, and files. "This is an extremely small space. We had to be inventive."

5 USE CURTAINS STRATEGICALLY
The low-ceilinged master bedroom (actually a sleeping loft above the living area) has curtains that conceal bedside tables and a large storage area. "Even though there's the sense that the apartment is bigger than it is, that's not important to me. I like small spaces."

6 COLOR CONTINUITY
Using the same mustard and blue hues throughout ensures that the look doesn't veer too busy—and that everything looks of a piece.

7 DISGUISE THE KITCHEN
Folding doors dressed in geometric-print wallpaper hide the galley kitchen that runs the length of the entry hall—about 12 feet. "Creating folding doors allowed us to transform the entry into a mini gallery when we entertain," says Brockschmidt.

8 BE REALISTIC "I cook when we have a party, but not on a daily basis, so we didn't need fancy appliances—we needed narrow appliances!" the designer explains. Simple white Ikea cabinets were given a decorative flourish with a Directoire-style diamond pattern in the same Mustard Olive as the walls.

PHOTOGRAPHY CREDITS

William Abranowicz/ Art + Commerce: 28, 105 top left

Gordon Beall: 80

James Carrière: 86

Roger Davies: 14

Reed Davis: 62 left

François Dischinger: 131 top left

Brian Doben: 51, 70, 82 left, 110–111

Miki Duisterhof: 53 bottom left, 78 bottom right

Pieter Estersohn: 109 top left

Sam Gray: 106 left

Gridley + Graves: 74

Mick Hales: 49 top, 102

Alec Hemer: 16 top, 50, 61, 131 bottom right, 144

Bob Hiemstra: 130

Ditte Isager/Edge Reps: 42, 113, 115, 125

John Kernick: 141

Francesco Lagnese: 18, 49 bottom right, 53 top, 57 bottom left and right, 62 right, 128, 143 bottom right

Thomas Loof: 16 bottom, 26 right, 32–33, 34, 35, 38, 54 left, 58, 60 left, 63, 64–65 (Statue of Liberty in snow © Landon Nordeman), 66, 67, 68, 69, 72, 82 right, 85 bottom, 100, 118, 143 top left and right, 143 bottom left, 145 top, 147

Maura McEvoy: 30

James Merrell: 24, 25, 93 (both), 139 top right

Karyn Millet: 78 top right

Ngoc Minh Ngo: 6, 17 bottom right, 26 left, 31, 40, 60 right, 81, 106 right, 107, 109 top right, 117, 135 right, 148 right

Peter Murdock: 78 bottom left, 94–95, 96, 97 (both)

Amy Neunsinger: 46–47, 48, 140

Victoria Pearson: 2, 10, 17 top left, 27 bottom, 43, 49 bottom left, 57 top, 78 top left, 84 bottom left, 116, 132, 133, 149

Eric Piasecki: 4, 79, 83, 85 top, 104, 142

José Picayo: 12

Paul Raeside: 131 top right

Lisa Romerein: 8, 29, 92 right, 134, 139 bottom left

Mark Roskams: 87, 136–137

Annie Schlechter: 52, 135 left

Nathan Schroder: 19, 54 right

Tim Street-Porter: 109 bottom right

Eric Striffler: 53 bottom right

Trevor Tondro: 88, 92 left, 105 top right, 108, 109 bottom left

Luca Trovato: 27 top, 37, 56 right, 145 bottom

Jonny Valiant: 13, 17 top right, 17 bottom left, 20–21, 44, 45, 56 left, 59 (all photos), 77 right, 84 bottom right, 99, 138, 139 top left, 139 bottom right

Björn Wallander: 15, 23, 55, 90, 114, 146

Julian Wass: 11, 76, 84 top, 126, 131 bottom left, 148 left

Simon Watson: 75, 89, 91 (both), 105 bottom right, 119, 120–121, 122, 123 (all photos), 150–151, 152 (both), 153 (both)

FRONT JACKET: Alec Hemer

FRONT INSIDE FLAP: Shutterstock

BACK JACKET (clockwise from top left): Luca Trovato, Ngoc Minh Ngo, Eric Piasecki

BACK JACKET (bottom left): Artwork by © Hiroshi Sugimoto, courtesy Fraenkel Gallery, San Francisco and Pace Gallery, New York

FRONT AND BACK COVER: Luca Trovato

SPINE: Lara Robby/ Studio D

HEARST BOOKS
New York

An Imprint of Sterling Publishing
387 Park Avenue South
New York, NY 10016

Every effort has been made to ensure that all the information in this book is accurate. However, due to differing conditions, tools, and individual skills, the publisher cannot be responsible for any injuries, losses, and/or other damages that may result from the use of the information in this book.

ISBN 978-1-61837-132-4

Distributed in Canada by Sterling Publishing
c/o Canadian Manda Group, 165 Dufferin Street
Toronto, Ontario, Canada M6K 3H6

Distributed in the United Kingdom by GMC Distribution Services
Castle Place, 166 High Street, Lewes, East Sussex, England BN7 1XU

Distributed in Australia by Capricorn Link (Australia) Pty. Ltd.
P.O. Box 704, Windsor, NSW 2756, Australia

For information about custom editions, special sales, and premium
and corporate purchases, please contact Sterling Special Sales at 800-805-5489
or specialsales@sterlingpublishing.com.

Manufactured in China

2 4 6 8 10 9 7 5 3 1

www.sterlingpublishing.com